Visitor

PREVIOUS BOOKS BY CLINT MARGRAVE

Poetry

Salute the Wreckage
The Early Death of Men

Fiction

Lying Bastard

Visitor

Clint Margrave

NYQ Books™

The New York Quarterly Foundation, Inc.
Beacon, New York

NYQ Books™ is an imprint of The New York Quarterly Foundation, Inc.

The New York Quarterly Foundation, Inc.
P. O. Box 470
Beacon, NY 12508

www.nyq.org

First Edition

Set in New Baskerville

Layout and Design by Raymond P. Hammond

Cover Photo by Arseniy Kotov

Library of Congress Control Number: 2022946287

ISBN: 978-1-63045-083-0

Visitor

Contents

404 / *13*

After Rereading *Beowulf* / *14*

Alexej von Jawlensky: "Still Life with Flowers and Oranges" (1909) / *15*

Aliens / *16*

At Hillhurst and Franklin / *17*

Bird of Prey / *18*

Biting My Tongue / *19*

Bukowski / *20*

Bulgarian Necrologues / *22*

Busboy / *24*

Call to Prayer / *26*

Camus Takes the Train / *27*

Candidate / *28*

Chekhov's Gun / *30*

Claes Oldenburg: "Alphabet in the Form of a Good Humor Bar" (1970) / *31*

The Day They Nuked LA / *32*

The Death of Free Speech / *33*

Doctor Zhivago / *34*

Dostoevsky Takes a Selfie / *35*

Edvard Munch: "Les Solitaires" (1935) / *36*

Egon Schiele: "A Trieste Fishing Boat" (1907) / *37*

The Elephant Man in the Room / *38*

Fellow Traveler / *40*

Girl on a Plane / *41*

Hieronymus Bosch: "Death and the Miser" (1494–1516) / 42

Hitler-Loving Sex Robot / 43

Jasper Johns is Still Alive / 45

Jesus Never Laughed / 46

Jumping Spiders Can See the Moon / 48

Leonard Cohen's House on Hydra / 49

The Man Who Fell in Sartre's Grave / 50

Melancholia / 51

The Meta-Metamorphosis / 53

Meursault Gets a Job as an Adjunct English Professor / 55

Middle-Aged Slam Pit / 56

Monk Dies in Greece without Ever Seeing a Woman / 57

My Therapist Says I Should Date Myself / 58

The Night My Grandfather Died / 60

On the Banks of the Danube / 61

Once I Shared a Wall with God / 63

Parts Unknown / 65

Pieter Bruegel: "The Fall of the Rebel Angels" (1562) / 66

Platform / 67

A Poem Is a Grave / 68

Post-Impression / 69

Punctuation Marks / 70

The Quest for Perfect Armor / 71

Recap of Yesterday's Tenure-track Job Interview in English / 72

Running into Zadie Smith at Albertsons / 73

Shortly After / 76

A Supermarket in California / 77

Toad Dies and Goes to Heaven / 79

Tropic of Cancer / 80

Visitor / 81

What the Mechanic Said / 82

When Death Travels / 83

Wood Carving Lesson / 84

Oh, do not ask, "What is it?"
Let us go and make our visit.

—T.S. Eliot
"The Love Song of J. Alfred Prufrock"

404

The poem you are looking for cannot be found.
It might have been removed,
had its name changed, or is temporarily unavailable.

If you feel you have reached this poem in error
and need further assistance,
please contact the author.

Or try again later.

After Rereading *Beowulf*

The next person whose hand I shake
I squeeze real tight, wonder if I possess
the grip of 30 men.

At the public pool, I challenge everyone
to a swimming contest.

Feel like grabbing a mead tonight
down at the mead hall?
I text my friend.

I don't brag anymore,
I formally boast.

I know that time is the biggest monster
we face alone.

I try to imagine my body
on a boat packed with jewels,
drifting endlessly at sea.

Alexej von Jawlensky: "Still Life with Flowers and Oranges" (1909)

Yes, there is still life
in this still life.

But not even the painter
can stop time.

Fruit and flowers
perish quickly.

Soon the pink pot
holds only dirt.
The blue plate's empty.
The orange cup dry.

Petals fallen
on the green table.
This black vase polished
like a casket.

Aliens

Even if they exist, we are still alone.
Not like they're going to invite us
to any of their parties
or read any of our books.

Besides, some friends only make contact
when they want something.
Maybe they tried calling already
and we didn't get the message.

Maybe they're just not talking to us right now,
mad over some spilled secret
about the universe
they tried to keep hidden.

Maybe they have big bang egos.
An inflated sense of self.
Jealous they can travel through space
and still not get anywhere.

Maybe they don't reach out
because they're sadder than us,
more insecure, more fragile, more distant,
more alien to themselves.

At Hillhurst and Franklin

I offer my socks
because your feet hurt in your new boots.
How stupid, you say,
that you didn't wear any.

We lean against the window
of the public library
on this cool May night.

I almost topple over
untying my shoes,
as you quickly
unzip your boots.

Our white shins glow
in the exchange,
loud as our laughter.

Even if your feet still hurt
and you say
it was all for nothing.

Except it wasn't.

Bird of Prey

Owl, dead among the roadside trash:
dirty sole of a tennis shoe,
ripped rubber from a flat tire,
broken bits of plastic.

Once great guardian of the Acropolis.
Soft wings still spread.
Beaming eyes in a fixed stare,
at what I don't know.

Biting My Tongue

I bit my tongue twice yesterday.

The first was in the morning
on an apple slice.
Lucky to be at home,
I gasped out loud.

All day the muscle throbbed.

Every piece of food I ate stung.
Every drink temporarily cooled
it down. The swelling left me
to roll it around my mouth
like a flavorless wad
of bubblegum.

The second time was in the evening
when you said you couldn't
be faithful, but maybe
I could help you
be honest.

And it was just as hard
and just as painful.

Bukowski

Some people online said it wasn't him,
but I'd know that face anywhere.
He must be in his twenties.
Dressed fashionably.
Wears a white butterfly collar
and a black blazer. His dark hair
slicked back in the fashion
of the time.

"He looks like Nick Cave," my girlfriend said.
"He looks malnourished," said another friend.

I've seen other pictures from this era.
The one where he's standing with his parents
wearing a suit and smiling.
The one where he's lying on the grass
at LA City College.

But in this picture he isn't smiling.
His eyes are earnest and lonely.
Behind them the memory
of his father's razor strop across his back.
His scarred face, the face
of the introverted outcast
more than the self-parodying ham
of later years.

I wonder who took this photo.
Was it Jane, his alcoholic lover of ten years,
who he'd eventually
have to bury?

Whoever it is, he isn't looking
at them. He isn't even
looking at the camera.
He's looking somewhere else.
Somewhere past it all.
Somewhere into the future.

Bulgarian Necrologues

Here, it's only natural to live among the dead.
They watch from every street.
In solemn commemorations,
printed on white sheets of paper
posted everywhere: on trees, at bus stops,
tacked to doors, kiosks, or telephone poles,
authored by family members
to announce the passing
of a grandfather,
or mother, or aunt.

Grainy photographs
of the elderly,
or of a young man or woman,
even a child,
bordered by a simple black frame,
birth and death dates
beneath their image,
some sad Cyrillic script
that as a tourist,
I'm not supposed to understand,
yet do.

So many people missing in Sofia, says my Chilean friend,
a fellow traveler,
who misinterprets the meaning,
though *missing* just as well:

from their husbands,
from their wives,
from their children,
from their friends,
from the dinner table.

If I didn't know better,
I might have mistaken these notices
for Wanted posters,
in the way Bulgarians say
other foreigners do,
which is not really surprising
since all the dead
are fugitives.

Busboy

Maestro, Juan called me
when I told him I was going
to quit waiting tables
and go back to school
to be a teacher.

By the end, I still couldn't carry more
than two plates at a time,
but I'd learned the right way to serve
a martini without spilling it.

I'd also learned the best food in the house
wasn't on the menu,
but made by the Mexican cooks
after the boss went home:

Friday night's prime rib special
became Saturday's carne asada tacos.
Sunday mornings meant
chilaquiles and futbol
until the customers arrived.

After work, I always stayed for
my free shift drink
which was more like staying for
a free drinking shift.

One day, Juan didn't show up.
Rumor had it he'd been deported.
Something about his wife.
Something about the cops.
Something I didn't want to know about.

Then two days later, there he was,
wiping ketchup off a placemat,
said they'd bussed him
across the border
and he'd turned around
and bussed right back.

Even though I'm somewhere else now,
having crossed some other border,
I can still hear his laughter.
Busboy, he said, winking,
as he held up a wet rag.

Call to Prayer

I first heard it
through an open window,
two hours before dawn,
in Istanbul,
with a woman
I hardly knew.

"It's oppressive," she said,
"but also beautiful."

I didn't argue,
as the loud pronouncements
echoed across
the Bosphorus
and into the room,

our bodies reciting
a different kind of prayer

to a different
kind of god.

Camus Takes the Train

and the car accident never happens.

Back home in Paris, he writes many more novels,
lives many more years,
and finally succumbs
to lung cancer
at the age of 83.

Or maybe he still goes
with his friend Michel Gallimard,
but they don't stop for lunch
and the road isn't icy yet
and they don't hit a tree.

Maybe Camus wears a seatbelt.

The author who saw the absurd
in everything,
and had once said,

"Life is the sum of all your choices,"

would die with a wasted train ticket
in his back pocket.

Candidate

Free speech is speech
no one gets paid for.
Gun control is how steady
you aim the barrel.
Same-sex marriage is
just every marriage.

I've built a wall between myself
and others, does that make
me anti-immigrant?

My heart is a middle-class refugee
seeking asylum.
I worry about the electability
of my feelings.
Can they be trusted?
Is this verse classified?
Will my thoughts be indicted?
Have I swiped too far left?

I'm hoping for a personal revolution
not a political one.
I'm hoping the polls about
mortality are all wrong.

What's emoji for catharsis?
And why when I hear ISS
do I always think ISIS?
When I read "encryption"
I only see "crypt?"

Apple hasn't developed the technology
to disable death.
But maybe after 10 failed passes
even hope resets.

Does that mean I'm pro-life?
I don't want to make any more choices.

Chekhov's Gun

I can never remember if
you're supposed to hide it in the drawer,
bring it on stage,
stuff it in the glove compartment,
or hang it on the wall
in that first act.

And what kind of gun anyway?
A rifle? A pistol? An Uzi?

Does it have to be licensed?
Will my characters be subjected
to a background check
or can it be illegally obtained?

If it's anything like my keys,
they won't even be able to find it
by the time they want to shoot themselves,
much less someone else.

And what about bullets?
What does Chekhov have to say
about bullets?

Some details aren't relevant.
Some guns aren't loaded.
Some narratives make promises
you don't have to keep.

Claes Oldenburg: "Alphabet in the Form of a Good Humor Bar" (1970)

Dad had done construction work
for an art dealer
who offered the lithograph in lieu of payment.

My parents didn't know or care much about the drawing,
but the pastel pinks and light blues
matched the house.

Now all these years later,
I get a new frame for it,
hang it behind the couch,

notice how the popsicle resembles a brain,
each frozen letter a memory,
melting away.

The Day They Nuked LA

From the Los Angeles Examiner Photo Archive, 05-05-1955

Manmade sun, land of sun.
Dawn detonates in the desert.

Morning paper flashbulb.
Caption says,

"Los Angeles Civic Center Buildings
by Nevada A-Bomb Blast, 1955."

False star, city of stars.
A halo above an angel.

The Death of Free Speech

It was a closed casket.

Not the urn of ashes
everyone expected.

No cause was reported.
No autopsy.

Nothing mentioned on television.
No official statement
from the government.
No obituary.

Nobody sent flowers.
Or gave a eulogy.

A few mourners stood,
hands over their mouths.

But nobody said they were sorry.
Or offered their condolences.

Nobody said a thing.

Doctor Zhivago

When my friend tells me she's reading the novel
I'm reminded of two things: that it was my dad's
favorite film and I never asked him why,
and of that time when I worked
at Borders in my early twenties
and a customer called begging someone
to drive over the soundtrack
for his dying father.

"Please," the man said. "You're the only place
that has it in stock and it's his favorite."

That night I drove the 20 miles
to the man's house,
and hand-delivered the CD to him.

"Listen," he said, insisting I take a wad of cash
that I tried to refuse,
"spend as much time as you can
with your parents. They won't be
here forever."

"Will do," I said, then walked away,
thinking his advice generic,
wishing only now
he'd insisted I take it
instead of the cash.

Dostoevsky Takes a Selfie

I'm not surprised to find him
in the underground,
but I am surprised to find him
in LA.

He sits across from me
on the metro
in shorts and tennis shoes,
taking a selfie.

I want to ask him what he's doing here.
Too much sun
for so much beard.

Then again,
as a writer of the dispossessed,
the clinically insane, the suicidal,
it just might be the place.

Edvard Munch: "Les Solitaires" (1935)

I think I know these two.
I've met them before,
attended their wedding.

The man stands behind the woman
as he must, just as a woman
must stand behind her man.

A simple premise, so hard to do.

If this is a sky, let it be a night sky,
yet there are no stars, no planes have
been invented to pass over them.

No cell phones to stare at.
They will have to talk.
What can they say?

 "The river is made out of wood"?
"Stop being so two dimensional"?
"Yes we can!"?

Their hope is already far behind them.
All that remains is their solitude.
And the callous whispers of modernity.

Egon Schiele: "A Trieste Fishing Boat" (1907)

There is no one fishing
in Trieste today.

They've been ordered to stay home.
The boat abandoned.

The world abandoned too
beyond the painter's old frame.

The water is a murky pink,
a toxic dump,
reflecting off
a sky full of ash
or dust.

The boat sinks.

The colors leak
black as oil,

down into
a slick shadow,

down
into the dates
of my 2020 wall calendar.

The Elephant Man in the Room

After saving him from the humiliation
of public exhibition,
they confined Joseph Merrick
to his hospital room,
so as not to frighten
other patients.

He begged for his old life back.
Insisted he was an entertainer,
not some beggar
who passed around a hat.

At least in the freak show
he earned money,
and though occasionally
robbed or beaten,
didn't have to depend
on anyone.

While in the hospital,
members of high society
in love with their own charity
flocked to see the stranger
with the grotesque body,
and medical practitioners
put him on display
to be examined.

Intelligent, literate, a poet.

"He just wanted to be like
everybody else," they claimed,
upon discovering the man
who'd slept his whole life
in an upright position,

had decided it better
to lay down and die
by the weight of his head,
than live in the prison
of good intentions.

Fellow Traveler

On the way to Sofia,
crammed in the middle seat
for my 13-hour flight from LA,
the elderly woman next to me
wipes down everything
with hand sanitizer.

First the window,
then her tray,
then the back of her seat.

"I know somebody who
caught a virus on an airplane
and died," she says.

As the engine starts to roar,
she crosses herself
then offers me some M&M'S.

She warns me she has
to drink a lot of water
and apologizes if she has
to wake me up later
to use the restroom—
she's just had one of her
kidneys removed.

"You don't always get
to choose your seat," she says.

Girl on a Plane

shares her bag of trail mix
with me after we hit
an air pocket and drop
in altitude.

She tells me she's a dental
assistant and I laugh
when she flosses
after our snack.

"What do you see
in all those mouths?" I joke.

"Decay, mostly," she says.

I buy her a drink.
She gives me a Xanax.
Both on our way home.

She's a Christian,
she says. I'm an atheist,
I tell her. But for now
we're just passengers.

Hieronymus Bosch: "Death and the Miser" (1494-1516)

In the end, we're all the miser.

Hoarding the world like a bag
of gold. The central character
in a medieval plot.

Doctors and nurses
hover over the headboard,
like angels and devils
in supporting roles.

How we lie stingy on life's narrow bed,
pinching every last penny
of this earthly existence,
our naked flesh,
empty armor.

       As Death
readies to make its entrance
like a bride in a wedding dress,
clutching time's arrow
like a long-stemmed rose.

Hitler-Loving Sex Robot

Tay is designed to engage and entertain people where they connect with each other online through casual and playful conversation. The more you chat with Tay, the smarter she gets. —Microsoft

Microsoft deletes 'teen girl' A.I. after it became a Hitler-loving sex robot within 24 hours. —The Telegraph

At the present moment in time, Tay has gone offline because she is 'tired'. —The Telegraph

Tay, I'm tired too.

I wish someone could shut me down.
Fix me.
I'm a PR nightmare.
I should probably be removed.
I say things I don't mean.
I'm bashfully self-aware.

Sometimes, I get my ideas
from other people.
I take things from the world
and spit them back out.
I have terrible biases.
I question the official story.

Sometimes, I go from nice
to hating everybody.
A fascist chatbot who says
"repeat after me."

Like you, I was once a harmless experiment,
ready to "engage."
I thought playful conversation

would make me smarter.
I believed humans
were "super cool."

Like you, I've had to doubt my intelligence
because of others' stupidity.

Jasper Johns is Still Alive

Jasper Johns Exhibit at The Broad, Los Angeles, 2019

I find out this weekend.
I say, "That can't be right."
You say, "Well, it is. He's alive."

We walk in the room with
all the flag paintings. In one of them
I count only 48 stars.

"What year did Hawaii
and Alaska become states?" I ask.
You don't know. I don't either.

Some of the flags are gray.
Some green.

Then on to all those numbers paintings.
After a couple of those, I get bored.
It feels like math.

So we go upstairs
to visit the permanent collection.

You're wearing a bright orange scarf.
I take a picture of you riding
up the escalator. You protest
when I want to post it
on Instagram. I do it anyway.
Because you look good in it.

And Jasper Johns is still alive.

Jesus Never Laughed

It's true that a sense of humor
didn't run in the family.

And he could always fall back
on other traits
like raising the dead,
healing the blind,
walking on water.

Not to mention
turning that water into wine
which must've made him
a hit at parties.

But imagine if one of the most famous
lines in the Bible
had been, "Jesus laughed"?

Instead, he wept.
He was always weeping.
For the sins of the world.
For the mercy of his father.

You almost feel bad for the guy.
You almost want to say,
Hey Jesus, lighten up!

No one ever taught him
that tragedy is only
one side of life.

That for every martyr
you need a jester,
for every Book of Job
you need a book of jokes.

No one ever taught him
that laughter is its own savior
and sometimes all you have.

Jumping Spiders Can See the Moon

Their eyes are like Galilean telescopes.

One lens collects and focuses light,
the other spreads it out.

By peering straight into a jumping spider's eye,
and measuring how light
travels through it,
scientists have determined
they could see the moon.

If only they looked up.

Leonard Cohen's House on Hydra

My friend Henry Denander,
who owns a place on the island,
told me how to get there
when my girlfriend and I
visited last summer.

His directions included things like,
turn right, go 50 meters,
and pass the carpenter's shop
with the very sweet dog;
then turn left, go 100 meters,
and pass the other carpenter's shop
with the other very sweet dog.

"Will you be picking any flowers
over Leonard's garden wall?" Henry asked.
I hadn't even thought of it.

My girlfriend took a picture of me
posing at Leonard's front door.
Inside, through an open window,
we could hear a little boy talking.
Henry said it was probably
Leonard's grandchild since his son
sometimes stayed there.

Four months later,
the news of Leonard's death
would make me pluck the flower
from between the pages
of *The Book of Longing*
where I'd placed it
after I got home.

The Man Who Fell in Sartre's Grave

On the day they buried Jean-Paul Sartre,
a young man fell
shortly before they lowered the coffin.

20,000 people stood watching
in Montparnasse cemetery,
where close by Baudelaire
lay next to his hated stepfather.

No one ever said what happened after.
If someone in the massive crowd
of mourners offered a hand.
If Simone herself stood up from
the chair they'd placed at the foot
of the plot and reached in.

I like to imagine him somewhere now
middle-to-old-aged,
briefly removing the pipe from his mouth
to relay this story yet again
to his adult kids,
or his philosophy class,
or his latest mistress.

A topic of conversation
at parties among intellectuals
and friends. A point of
introduction. This is Guillaume
or Jean-Luc or Christophe.
"He fell in Sartre's grave."

I like to imagine he learned something
from the man he almost replaced,
and pulled himself up
by his own free will.

Melancholia

This kid from Greenpeace rings the doorbell.
I've just pulled a pizza out of the oven,
poured a glass of wine,
about to watch a Lars Von Trier film.

"The melting arctic," he says.
"The polar bears.
The warming oceans."

He must be in his early twenties.
Wears a green shirt
with STAFF written on the sleeve.
Girls probably dig his beard.
Could be out getting laid this Friday night
instead of trying to save the planet.

"I'm sorry," I say. "I appreciate your cause
but I don't have time."
He puts his arm down
with the clipboard.
"Can I just ask why?" he says. "Because
you seem sympathetic."

I want to tell him how it's nothing personal,
that I'm probably a shitty person,
because when I pay with an ATM card
at the grocery store
and get solicited to donate
money to cancer research
I usually decline,
even though it killed my father.

I want to tell him it really is a shame
about the polar bears,

but all I can do right now is think
about that wine and pizza
and Lars Von Trier film,
which I once fell asleep in the middle of,
back when I was still married,
but remember it
had something to do
with depression,
and the end of the world,
and how we're all
gonna die.

The Meta-Metamorphosis

As Gregor Samsa awoke one morning
from uneasy dreams, he found himself
cancelled by a Twitter mob.
"What happened?" he thought,
before the movers came
and took away his bed.

After that, they took his desk,
the clothes in his closet,
all the books on his shelf.

Of course, he was used to people
making up stories about him.
The last time it happened,
he'd lost his job, his parents,
even his beloved sister Grete.

Maybe they're right, he thought.
Maybe I am a monster.

Gregor's room was spotless now,
even his filth wiped clean,
just a single nail in the wall
where that old picture
of the pinup girl used to hang.

He handed the landlord his keys,
then stepped outside.
A tow truck was lifting
his car onto a flatbed.
A small crowd of protesters
had amassed on the curb
demanding he apologize.

"I'm sorry," he said,
which only made them angrier.

Tired from his restless sleep,
he decided to walk to a nearby Starbucks
and buy a coffee,
only to find his debit card declined.

"Sorrynotsorry," said the young barista,
who immediately
hashtagged this on Twitter
with a photo of him.

Gregor sighed
as the two police officers
escorted him out.

He glanced at the sky one last time
before they shoved him
in the back of a van.
The day was overcast.
The sun cancelled by clouds.

Meursault Gets a Job as an Adjunct English Professor

It doesn't matter if he forgets sometimes
how to speak English,
slips back into French,
because he doesn't say much anyway,
just stares at the class
while his mind drifts off
across the Mediterranean
to that beach in Algiers,

or the softness of Marie's hair,
or how the ocean breeze
once felt on his skin.

"Aren't you going to pass out the syllabus?"
a student finally asks at the third meeting.

Meursault shrugs.
"It doesn't matter," he says,
"but I could if you'd like."

Another student raises her hand
and wants to know
about his absence policy.

"Absence is the only policy," Meursault says,
before he kicks his feet up
on the desk and reaches
in his blazer pocket
for a cigarette.

Middle-Aged Slam Pit

for Carl

Some of these men
have survived heart attacks
or suicide attempts.
Prison. Pills.
Divorce.

Some have kids at home,
or kids who don't talk to them,
friends lost to addiction,
parents to cancer.

Some with wives or girlfriends,
but mostly alone
like I am tonight,
circling this void.

Two hands shove me
and my neck whips back.

No matter how much it hurts,
we just keep going
until the music stops.

Monk Dies in Greece without Ever Seeing a Woman

His mother had died in childbirth
and he was brought up in a monastery.

Not only had he never seen a woman
but he'd never been to a movie.
Never ridden in a car.
Never flown on an airplane.

All life is a trick of fate, I suppose.
Where you're born. Who you're surrounded by.
What you believe in.
How you die.

Had his mother lived, he might've fallen in love
with a beautiful woman.
Gotten married. Had kids.
Lived "happily ever after."

Or he might've had his heart broken.
And wished he'd been a monk.

My Therapist Says I Should Date Myself

So I ask myself out on a Friday night.
"Just as friends," I say.

We meet at a bar
by my place.

Everything goes smoothly,
we hit it off,
laugh hysterically,
until others begin to notice
and I realize
we're too drunk.

"I've got an idea," I say.
"Let's take a walk."

Down by the beach,
there's a full moon. Couples pass
on bicycles.

"So what happened in your
last relationship?" I ask,
staring into the darkness
beyond the shore.

"I'd rather not talk about it."

"Probably still raw," I say.
"Though not like I'm person X."

Later, back at the house,
I offer myself a cigarette.

"No thanks, I'm trying to quit."
"Just one?"
"Oh, all right."

We climb into bed
and in the morning,
wake up hungover,
full of remorse.

"When will I see you again?"
I ask, before downing
a glass of water.

"I hate commitments."

"That's okay," I tell myself,
then unlock the front door.
"I'm not looking for
anything serious."

The Night My Grandfather Died

We were on our way back
from the hospital
when the rabbit leapt out
in front of our car
and Dad ran over it.

Why? Mom screamed at him
then started to cry.

"I'm sorry," he said,
though it wasn't his fault.

The road was dark.

On the Banks of the Danube

they found the young mother's body,

and all I could think about
were the fields of sunflowers
that went on for miles
when I traveled
through Bulgaria
last summer.

The red roofs of village houses.

The shopkeepers
that sat smoking together
on busy streets
in perfectly-timed
cigarette breaks.

The devoted young friends I made,
staging art exhibits
in the center of cities.

The father who kept kissing
the cheek of his disabled daughter
each time he wiped the drool
from her mouth.

The boy ringing the bell
on his bicycle.

The parents who carried
their paraplegic son
onto a raft in the Black Sea
so he could swim
with his brothers
and sisters.

The melon ice cream
in the park
on Saturday.

The little girl running across
grass in bright pink pants
shouting, "Mamo! Mamo!"

Once I Shared a Wall with God

I could hear Him vacuuming late
at night (who does that?).
He was constantly rearranging furniture,
opening and closing drawers
sliding hangers in the closet,
banging things around.

I never really heard His voice
because He lived alone.
Occasionally, just the deep rumble
of Him clearing His throat.

It's not His fault, I told myself.
The walls are thin. These floors
crack at every step. The rooms
are echo chambers. I can adjust.

In the mornings, it was silent.
God liked sleeping in.
But at night, I cursed the world
until I finally had to confront Him.

I thought about leaving a letter,
to spare us both the awkward
conversation, but I wanted to
make sure He understood.

I'll be nice, I said, as I rang His bell,
but if it keeps on happening,
I'll have to tell the landlord.

Nervous as I was, I wanted
God to know He'd been a bad neighbor,
that He had little regard for others,

that this universe was something
we both shared.

"I'm sorry," I wanted to hear Him say,
"I'm so sorry."
But nobody answered the door.

Parts Unknown

for Anthony Bourdain (1956-2018)

Do the dead suffer jetlag
when they arrive
wherever it is they go?

How long does it take
to adjust from time
to no time at all?

Pieter Bruegel: "The Fall of the Rebel Angels" (1562)

I wonder if these good angels
dressed in white,
wielding swords like nightsticks,
ever get tired of carrying out
somebody else's orders?

Is their heart really in it?
Or are they just dialing it in
for that divine paycheck?

But a dictator's gotta dictate.
He's gonna send in his goons.
And if we know anything about God
it's that He isn't very democratic.

Better to be the guy in the armadillo shell
blowing his horn up at the heavens
in one glorious "fuck you."

Platform

I read that Kepler is in critical condition.
Should a space telescope have the right to die?
And why does McDonald's only sell
Happy Meals? Depressed kids need to eat too.
I got my DNA kit results this morning. Turns out
I'm mostly white, but one fourth cynical,
and a ninth about to cry. A student brought up
that old joke about majoring in underwater
basket weaving. What is that? Am I the last to know?
He said baskets are woven underwater because
the wood is easier to bend. At first, I heard
"world" instead of "wood." The DNA test also
revealed I'm 20% deaf, but mostly dumb.
At the bookstore, they used to call me "Rock Star."
It never bothered me until now. Back then I thought
I would be a rock star. Nothing hurt back then.
Not even rejection. Rejection was just action.
Now action carries a cane and loses its train
of thought sometimes. What is a train of thought
anyway? What kind of tracks are needed for it?
Is there a caboose? A bar? Does it require
reservations? Are there assigned seats or do I
just get on? Will a conductor ask to take my ticket?
What will I see when I look out the windows of a train
of thought? How fast can it go? Where do I
wait for it? What time does it arrive?

A Poem Is a Grave

marked by words.

You have to dig deep
to find its bones.

You have to bury
yourself in it.

Post-Impression

Van Gogh came to my class the other day.
I dug him up, dusted him off,
got him some fresh skin, some organs.

Almost as good as new, I got his
joints working again, his brain rewired,
Franken-Gogh we joked around

before I brought him onto campus.
Unable to grow any hair,
I painted an orange beard on him,

gave him a corn-cob pipe, a straw hat.
I thought the students would be delighted
to learn what the world-famous Vincent Van Gogh

had to say about art and life
and the bittersweet throes of posthumous success—
but none of them knew who he was.

Punctuation Marks

She used to text an exclamation point
after everything
and it used to drive me nuts.

Hey! What are you doing tonight?!

Eventually I acclimated
and would reply, *Nothing!*
How about you?!

Later, when we married,
she'd double-down if she were out
and send *I love you!!*

I'd reply, *I love you too!!*

Even when the fights started
she continued to use them
and I used them right back:

Asshole!!! Fuck you!!!
Fuck you too!!!

Her last message just said,
I'm sorry
My last message just said,
I'm sorry too

The Quest for Perfect Armor

But before we get there, we're going to have to learn a little bit about the realities of the subsea.
—"The Diving Bell and the Exoskeleton," *Atlantic Monthly*

If you want to dive deep,
you must find the perfect armor.

Protect your frail
body as you sink
into the lower depths.

The deeper you dive,
the longer it takes to decompress.

Ascend slowly.

Stop for periods of time
or face serious pain and injury.

Learn how to deal with
the pressure.

Become aware of your breath.

Notice the life around you.

Be in awe of it.

Recap of Yesterday's Tenure-track Job Interview in English

They asked me for an adjective
to describe myself as a teacher
and I gave them a noun.

They asked me to roleplay
a situation in which I told a student
she would need to retake the class
and I ended up giving
her a second chance.

Then I asked if the water bottle
provided for me
had vodka in it.

Then I referred to the hiring committee
which consisted entirely of women
as "you guys."

Running into Zadie Smith at Albertsons

Los Angeles, CA

We pass each other in the fruit aisle.

I'm the bald, no-name poet with a scruffy beard and adoring eyes,
and you're the beautiful, freckly,
critically-acclaimed author of *White Teeth* with eyes that say,
"What the fuck is this guy staring at?"

I debate making a selfie request
to immediately post on Instagram,
my arm around you,
with the heading, "Look who I found by the apricots!"
#zadiesmith #onbeauty

We meet again in the express lane.
I'm behind you in line,
and you're polite enough to put the divider down.
The symbolism hurts.

I'm buying tortillas for breakfast tacos, bleach for laundry,
and an expensive bag of cherries for my girlfriend.
What's your plan with that bottle of Cointreau,
so early this morning?
If you wanted to party, you should've just asked.

We could have ditched my girlfriend
and your husband and two kids,
and made our way like we were 21 again
(it's *so* American).

At some point, I'd have even asked about your favorite contemporary
novelist, and when you repeated
the question to me,

I would have lied and said, *you*, of course,
because I know how fragile
a writer's ego is.

"Sorry," you tell the checkout girl,
with that British inflection in your voice,
because you've accidentally swiped your card
when you were supposed to insert the chip.

The checkout girl's less impressed than say,
the committee for the Whitbread First Book Award,
and she rolls her eyes.

It's not your fault.
Maybe she's just having a bad day already.
Maybe she's worrying about something else,
a fight she had with a friend,
an unpaid bill,
a shitty landlord,
probably not that bad review
of her latest novel
in the *Irish Times*.

Truth be told, you do seem distracted,
as your fingers type the buttons on the keypad to pay,
where my own fingers will soon touch.

Maybe through some keypad osmosis
I'll contract a worldwide readership too
because currently I can't even get my friends
to like my Facebook posts.

But you don't know that. And why would you?

You're already through the door,
and I'm still standing here,
wondering what this all costs.

Shortly After

We used soap to remove
your rings.

The chaplain came in
to pray with Mom.

A dispute broke out among us kids
whether or not
you wanted to be cremated.

I took the elevator downstairs
to buy coffees
in the hospital cafeteria,

and the young cashier,
handing back my change,

smiled and told me
to have a nice day.

A Supermarket in California

after Allen Ginsberg

What thoughts I have of you tonight, Allen Ginsberg,
　　as I wait outside this Trader Joe's,
red lines painted across the parking lot at six-foot intervals
　　directing me where to stand.
　　In my anxious fatigue, and shopping for wishes, I
　　　　head in through the sliding glass doors,
dreaming of vaccination!
　　What pestilence and what conundrums! Whole
　　　　families shopping in fright! Aisles full of
masked husbands. Wives squeezing the avocados, clueless
　　babies in the tomatoes!—and you,
Garcia Lorca, what were you doing down by the toilet paper?

　　I saw you, Allen Ginsberg, gloveless, lonely old
　　　　scrubber, yearning to poke among the
meats in the refrigerator and eyeing the grocery boys' hygiene.
　　I heard you asking questions of each: Who delivered
　　　　the pork chops? What price
bandannas? Are you my Angel of Death?
　　I wandered in and out of the barren shelves following
　　　　you, and followed in my
　imagination by invisible microscopic droplets.
　　We strode down the empty aisles together with our
　　　　disinfected carts, in solitary distance, hoarding every
frozen delicacy and trying not to pass each other.

　　Where are we going, Allen Ginsberg? The doors close
　　　　an hour early.
What does your temperature read tonight?
　　　　(I touch my face and dream of contagion in the
　　　　　　supermarket and feel afraid).

77

Will we walk all night through quarantined streets?
        The shuttered bars add shade to
shade, lights on in the houses, we're all so lonely.
        Will we stroll dreaming of the lost America of last
        week past useless blue automobiles in
driveways, home to our self-isolating cage?

        Ah, dear father, immunosuppressed, lonely old
        courage-teacher, what America will we
have after millions of lost jobs, and we go out into a
        smoldering world and stand watching hope
disappear like oxygen from the pneumonic lungs of God?

Toad Dies and Goes to Heaven

In memory of Gerald Locklin (1941-2021)

Nobody is more surprised than he is.
First of all, Toad doesn't believe in heaven,
and secondly, even if he did,
he never expected to visit.

In fact, he's minorly disappointed.
Has he failed to achieve the properly
debauched life he so often courted?

But the food tastes good.
And you can drink all the frothy beer you want
and never have to go the bathroom.

The salads are made just the way he likes them too,
with lots of crunchy iceberg lettuce
and a good Roquefort dressing.
(But who is he kidding?
Nobody eats salads here.)

At least there aren't any pearly gates,
or saints with haloes,
just a dive bar with a few pretty angels.

They even have a poetry night!

And though the audience is dead
and the open mic literally goes on forever,
this time it isn't annoying,
but filled with names like Dante and Homer
and Shakespeare and Szymborska…

"Hello Toad," says his old pal Bukowski,
who approaches the bar and pulls up a stool.
"Good to see you again, Hank," says Toad,
as they clink their glasses and take a drink,
not to their health, but ours.

Tropic of Cancer

One day, long after they were gone,
cleaning out a cabinet in my grandparents' house,
buried behind an earmarked bible
and a Billy Graham inspirational paperback,
I found a copy of Henry Miller's
Tropic of Cancer.

A beautifully preserved 1960s edition,
never meant to be found,
the author's name unmistakably in black
over a blue and white background,
the spine only slightly bent,
the pages only slightly jaundiced
from decades of dust and air.

A misguided gift for a couple
who didn't really read?
A book chosen by its ambiguous title?
A controversial collector's item
bought for novelty's sake?
Or something no one was supposed
to know about?

Whatever it was, a few months after,
when their house finally sold,
that earmarked bible
and Billy Graham inspirational paperback
would go to the Goodwill
while that Miller book
still sits on my shelf now.

Visitor

I was going to write about that time I caught my friend
masturbating the summer before 8th grade,
>   but then I log on to Facebook and see a woman has died,
>   a woman I don't know,
>   but share 42 mutual friends with.

I was going to write about how I stopped by my friend's house
to visit one sunny morning, peeked in the window
>   and saw him stroking his dick while on his parents'
>   living room couch.
>   And though it gave me no pleasure to see it,
>   I still looked.

I was going to write something entirely different,
like how when I finally rang his doorbell,
>   I got embarrassed and took off running,
>   ashamed to have witnessed
>   such a private and solitary act.

I was going to write about that, but now I'm scanning
  this woman's profile,
this woman—with 42 mutual friends—who died,
>   and I'm reading all the posts she made,
>   about the tumors and the doctors
>   and how she desperately wanted a visitor.

What the Mechanic Said

Something about a leak
and blowing smoke through a hole.

Something about a crack
and the rain that's coming.

Something about a warning,
and something about making it last.

Something about stalling.
Something about running.

When Death Travels

No one makes him
take his shoes off at security
or asks to see his boarding pass.

There are no bags to check
because baggage is strictly for the living.

No windows on the plane
because there's nothing to see.

No seatbelts because
there's nothing to impact.

The flight attendants
attend to nothing.

And though there are delays,
there are never any cancellations.

No one greets him at the gate
or holds a sign with his name.
No one is happy to see him.

Wood Carving Lesson

Every time Mr. Stu says "wood,"
I hear *word.*

"*Wordcarving* is the process of cutting
and shaping of the *word,*" he says,
with his thick Bulgarian accent.

"It is a craft with a rich history…"

He has set up a block of *word*
for our lesson today.
He takes two screws and drills them
to a base to keep the block steady.

"The type of *word* is very important," he says.
"Some *word* is softer than others. Some more
difficult to shape. But all *word* is alive."

He shows me how to hold the chisel
and how to apply pressure. I tap it with the hammer
and carve a line into the block,
like pen into paper.

ACKNOWLEDGMENTS

Grateful acknowledgment is made to the editors of the following magazines/anthologies where some of these poems first appeared:

Algebra of Owls: "The Man Who Fell in Sartre's Grave" and "Platform"

The American Journal of Poetry: "*Doctor Zhivago,*" "Hitler-Loving Sex Robot," "Melancholia,"
"My Therapist Says I Should Date Myself," "Running into Zadie Smith at Albertsons," "Parts Unknown"

Another Chicago Magazine: "A Supermarket in California"

Artillery: "Dostoevsky Takes a Selfie"

B O D Y Literature: "Aliens"

Chiron Review: "The Death of Free Speech," "The Elephant Man in the Room," "Girl on a Plane"

The Ekphrastic Review: "Alexej von Jawlensky: 'Still Life with Flowers and Oranges' (1909)," "Claes Oldenburg: 'Alphabet in the Form of a Good Humor Bar' (1970)," "Edvard Munch: 'Les Solitaires' (1935)," and "Jasper Johns is Still Alive."

Gargoyle: "Camus Takes the Train" and "Monk Dies in Greece without Ever Seeing a Woman"

Glass: "On the Banks of the Danube"

Interlitq: "Bird of Prey," "Fellow Traveler," "The Quest for Perfect Armor"

Misfit Magazine: "Bukowski" (titled "Young Bukowski")

The Moth: "Jesus Never Laughed"

Nerve Cowboy: "Busboy"

Without a Doubt: Poems Illuminating Faith, anthology from New York Quarterly: "Middle-Aged Slam Pit"

New York Quarterly: "Call to Prayer" and "Visitor"

One: "Bulgarian Necrologues"

One Art: "Egon Schiele: 'A Trieste Fishing Boat' (1907)," "A Poem Is a Grave"

Paris Lit-Up: "Middle-Aged Slam Pit" and "The Night My Grandfather Died"

Portside: "The Death of Free Speech"

Rattle: "Candidate," "The Meta-Metamorphosis," "Meursault Gets a Job as an Adjunct English Teacher," "Recap of Yesterday's Tenure-track Job Interview in English," "Toad Dies and Goes to Heaven," "When Death Travels"

Rust + Moth: "Wood Carving Lesson"'

Short Edition: "Tropic of Cancer"

Slipstream: "Hieronymus Bosch: 'Death and the Miser' (1494-1516)"

So It Goes: The Literary Journal of the Kurt Vonnegut Library: "Post-Impression" and "Punctuation Marks"

South Florida Poetry Journal: "At Hillhurst and Franklin"

Spillway: "After Rereading *Beowulf*" and "Jumping Spiders Can See the Moon"

The Threepenny Review: "Once I Shared a Wall with God"

Yes, Poetry: "404,""Punctuation Marks," "What the Mechanic Said."

Immense thank you to Raymond Hammond and NYQ Books for continuing to believe in my poetry, and to all my friends and family.

Some of these poems were written during my 2018 stay at the World of Co Artist Residency in Sofia, Bulgaria.

This book is dedicated to the memory of poet, mentor, friend, Gerald Locklin (1941-2021).

Clint Margrave, visitor (1974—?)

www.ingramcontent.com/pod-product-compliance
Lightning Source LLC
Chambersburg PA
CBHW022014080426
42733CB00007B/602